4 Essential Skills

for

Leaders, Managers & High Potentials

DEDICATION

This book is dedicated to *you* for all of the hard work and effort you put into making yourself better, helping others grow, and making a positive impact in your work environment and on your business results.

As you improve, so does the benefit you bring to your family and friends, both financially and emotionally. We at ManagingAmericans.com appreciate your efforts and are proud to be a part of *your success.*

A special thanks to our staff, especially our panel of Expert Business Leaders & Management Consultants, who provide unique and incredibly inspirational training articles each month.

Thank you to our families for supporting our education and careers throughout our lives & to my Mother, Annemarie for her tenacious effort to get me to "Write it down before you forget."

Everyone we meet as employees, managers and business leaders leave their mark on us; make us who we are. We acknowledge them for teaching us what we do not know, and following us when our time is right to lead.

I sincerely wish you a successful journey,
- Lisa Woods, President & CEO, ManagingAmericans.com

CONTENTS

HOW TO USE
THIS BOOK

This book defines Four Essential Skills necessary for leaders, managers and high potential professionals of all ages, backgrounds and job levels. It is designed as a tool to evaluate your current strengths, help you focus on areas that need improvement, identify actions needed to develop your skills, and learn from the progress you make as a result of your efforts by providing worksheets to document your actions & successes.

Writing down your activity is the best way to maintain the focus you need to succeed. The worksheets serve as a reminder to ensure successful actions become habits, and if you have a team, you can share your progress as a management tool to develop those skills in others.

Here Are 5 Steps To Getting The Most Out Of This Book:

1. Develop an understanding of the Four Essential Skills, what they mean, and why they are important.

2. Take the Self Assessment to identify your Strengths, as well as skills that can & should be improved upon.

   - The self assessment consists of 20 questions. You rate the percentage of time that each statement/question holds true. Questions are based on the Four Essential Skills outlined in the book and represent the outcome of your actions. It is important to answer based on how you believe you are perceived by others. Perception is reality.

   For Example: "I am consistent in my requests and expectations of others."
   This statement is true 0-20% of the time, 20-40%, 40-60%, 60-80%, or 80+% of the time?

   Some Things to Consider…
   - Share the Assessment Tool with your employees, peers and boss to see how they would rate you. This 360° skills review is a great way to get feedback and a perspective on how effective your efforts really are.
   - Have your employees take the Assessment for themselves and use it as a professional development tool for your entire team. Mentor them and support their efforts to improve.

3. Evaluate your results and Chart your Top Priorities.

   - Once you have completed the assessment, take the statements that rank in the 0%-20% range and transfer those to your TOP PRIORITY chart, followed by your 20%-40% statements. Don't worry about the rest; there will be time to improve those areas after tackling your critical issues.
   - On your TOP PRIORITY chart worksheet you will see a space for three actions you can take to improve your skills. Keep this section empty until you have completed reading PART TWO of the book.

4. Read through 100+ descriptions of actions you can take to improve your 4 Essential Skills.

   - As you read through, highlight the actions you feel comfortable implementing. Try to step outside of your comfort zone a little. You may be surprised at the positive results you can generate.
   - Once you've finished reading, go back and reference your TOP PRIORITY chart. Each action is linked to the questions in the assessment. Choose from the actions you have highlighted and add them next to your priorities. If you have other ways to improve, write them down and focus on implementing them over the coming weeks & months.

5. Chart your Progress including the actions that generated success and the responses resulting from your actions.
   - Included in this book is a Progress Report worksheet for each of the 4 Essential Skills. Whenever you see positive feedback from your action plan, write it down in your workbook.
   - Continue to reference your success until your behaviors become habits.
   - Use your learning experiences as teaching opportunities for your own employees.

We hope this book serves as a powerful tool to help you build the skills necessary to succeed in your career. Please take the time to read through the entire book in order to learn new skills, as well as refresh the ones you already do well. Remember, perception is reality. Judging yourself honestly, by the way you are perceived, not as you perceive yourself, is the most effective way to improve. Your results will be based on the effort you put into the process.

Good Luck!

PART ONE

DEFINITIONS AND
STARTING POINT

4 Essential Skills For Every Leader, Manager & High Potential

Take The Self Assessment

Chart Your Top Priorities

4 ESSENTIAL SKILLS FOR EVERY LEADER, MANGER & HIGH POTENTIAL

Taking a well-rounded approach to your professional development is the best way to ensure success both in today's job, and tomorrow's career. These skills will make work more enjoyable & fulfilling for yourself and those you encounter in your day-to-day life.

It does not matter if you are a company President, Operations Leader, Customer Service Representative, Sales & Marketing Director or "name your title"…the need for continuous self improvement is universal. Successful individuals make a proactive effort to continuously develop four Essential Skills to create a combined ability to *1. Lead, 2. Manage, 3. Perform in their Job & 4. Communicate Effectively.* This 4-pronged skillset applies to <u>your</u> job, no matter what your title or level in the hierarchy. If you strive to collectively improve in these four areas, you will improve the long-term aspects of your career, and the quality of your short-term results.

Why not focus on just one skill? You could, and that would bring you value, but each skill is related to one another. Together they will make you well rounded, able to solve problems and get things done.

The key is to address ALL FOUR Essential Skills; together they will make you a more effective professional. Read through all aspects of the 4-pronged skillset and ask yourself…Would I be happier and more fulfilled in my job if I had these abilities and generated these results?

Here are 4 Essential Skills for Every Leader, Manager & High Potential:

Skill #1   Leadership Ability

Why is *Leadership Ability* Crucial to Your Overall Professional Development?
Leadership is a soft skill that allows you to move forward, at your desired speed, in your career and in your personal life. It is essential in anyone's development whether you want to lead a business, department, team or your own destiny. It is about getting people to follow your lead & respect your input; this is vital no matter what you do.

Key Results:
- Others are interested in what you have to say.

- Others take action upon your request.
- You have clarity as to why things happen and what value you bring to the big picture.

Skill #2   Management Ability

Why is *Management Ability* Crucial to Your Overall Professional Development?
Whether you are currently a manger, or want to be one eventually, the ability to take on responsibly and coordinate multiple variables: people, processes, timelines, personalities, objectives, etc.... in order to get things done, is an essential aspect of your development.

Key Results:
- You develop a reputation for being reliable.
- You are able to create mutually beneficial relationships with others.
- You are able to get things done through effective collaboration.

Skill #3   Job Performance

Why is *Job Performance* Crucial to Your Overall Professional Development?
Being proficient, innovative, respected and resourceful in your job are all tangible skills necessary for your professional development. This, combined with your soft skills makes you a full package ready to advance in your career.

Key Results:
- Your work and efforts are known and respected.
- Your input is requested and valued by others.
- Your work is relevant within your organization and within your field of expertise.

Skill #4   Communication Skills

Why are *Communication Skills* Crucial to Your Overall Professional Development?
You can have great ideas, amazing abilities and productive relationships, but if you don't have the skill to communicate effectively, get buy in and mobilize others, you are limiting how much you can actually accomplish. Great Communication Skills give you an edge in everything you do as a manager, leader & individual contributor by understanding your audience and projecting your message in a way that others can understand, buy into and act upon.

Key Results:
- You are comfortable in your own skin no matter what the circumstance.
- You are able to work with others, no matter their personality, and feel accomplished.
- You are able to learn, understand concepts and use new information to improve yourself.

TAKE THE SELF ASSESSMENT

The ability to see yourself the way other people see you is an asset IF you have the willingness to use this insight as a tool for positive change. Focusing on what you want is not enough, by understanding how you are perceived, you can create a practical & productive action plan that achieves results.

This Essential Skills Self Assessment is the first step to finding out where you should target your efforts. The assessment will determine your strengths and weaknesses within the Essential Skillset, ultimately guiding you to what it takes for **you to be a Great Leader, Manager or Employee.**

The assessment is made up of 20-questions with 5 desirable results for each Essential Skill. You should rate yourself based on your CURRENT ability to achieve the desired result.

For example:
Result: I regularly get buy-in and approval for my ideas.
Your answer: I achieve this result 20-40% of the time.

Ideally you would prefer to get buy-in and approval for your ideas 80+% of the time, right? This would be an area that needs improvement. Once you define the areas that need improvement, you can identify your actions for professional growth. Part two of this book details the actions you can take to get there, but first focus on the assessment to create your foundation for positive change.

Your Mindset For Taking The Self Assessment...
When you answer the questions, imagine looking in a mirror, but instead of seeing what your ego sees, try to describe how others see you. How would your employees, your peers or your boss describe you? How would your customers describe you? Would you describe yourself the same way, or would there be conflicting perspectives? In the event of conflict, for the purpose of this assessment, we recommend you go with the OTHER person's perspective. When conducting a practical self-assessment, reality is in the eye of the beholder. Your ability to reflect and understand how others perceive your actions and abilities is a foundational communication skill that will allow you to grow and improve in other areas. That is why this self-assessment, done properly, is so important to your success. If you can truly identify your strengths and weaknesses, you will be able to focus on goals that not only improve your professional growth, but will also impact your professional success.

This exercise requires you to choose the "closest" percentage of agreement. If you can't decide...round down.

My **Leadership** Ability

Over the past 12 months what percentage of time does each statement hold true?	0% to 20%	20% to 40%	40% to 60%	60% to 80%	80% to 100%
My Direct Employees are interested in, and act on what I say.					
My Peers/Co-Workers are interested in, and act on what I say.					
My Boss is interested in, and acts on what I say.					
My objectives are known AND understood by everyone in the organization.					
Throughout my organization I can articulate the objectives of others and how well those objectives support my own.					

My **Management** Ability

Over the past 12 months what percentage of time does each statement hold true?	0% to 20%	20% to 40%	40% to 60%	60% to 80%	80% to 100%
I am consistent in my requests and expectations of others.					
I give praise to others for their accomplishments BOTH privately and publically.					
I understand the overall company goals and have created a clear action plan for myself and/or my team to support that effort.					
I am able to work across departmental silos to get things done and get the support needed to accomplish my team member objectives.					
I regularly provide constructive feedback and set both group & individual continuous improvement targets for my team.					

My **Job** Performance

Over the past 12 months what percentage of time does each statement hold true?	0% to 20%	20% to 40%	40% to 60%	60% to 80%	80% to 100%
I proactively implement new & improved ways of doing things on a regular basis.					
I am the go-to person for my area of expertise, in and outside of my department.					
I take on leadership roles for projects outside of my current job duties.					
I know the processes and people that interact with my area of responsibility both before and after my job takes place in the business cycle.					
I spend more time focusing on perfecting my current job vs. proving my ability for the position I really want to get promoted to.					

My **Communication** Skills

Over the past 12 months what percentage of time does each statement hold true?	0% to 20%	20% to 40%	40% to 60%	60% to 80%	80% to 100%
I regularly get buy-in and approval for my ideas.					
I am able to comfortably express myself using multiple communication vehicles (writing, presentations, discussions).					
I can properly articulate the concepts of others, and often do so to help them get buy-in for their ideas.					
I routinely share information, both good and bad, with the intent to engage others, solve problems and continuously improve.					
I proactively engage everyone in the company with positive dialog no matter their reaction or response.					

CHART YOUR TOP PRIORITIES

Focusing on the right things to succeed requires the ability to choose what NOT to work on today. Take the time now to chart your path with Top Priorities. Once you improve these skills, your priorities will change. That's the time to adjust, but for now…stay focused.

Congratulations on completing your Essential Skills Self Assessment. The next step is to review your results and identify where you should be focusing your time to develop your skills.

Review Your Results

Here is a breakdown of how to view your results based on your response to each individual question:

I achieve this result 0-20% of the time.
This is a Critical Issue to address; your current results are holding you back from success. Consider these results as your first priorities to focus on. You will have to make some radical changes in your actions; the positive improvements you achieve will be equally radical.

I achieve this result 20-40% of the time.
You have the ability to use this Essential Skill, however you are probably not comfortable using it based on different circumstances or people. Your goal is to step outside of your comfort zone with the tools you need to be confident and show your skills.

I achieve this result 40-60% of the time.
You already exhibit aspects of this Essential Skill, however your actions are probably not consistent. Once you create a greater awareness of the actions you should take, you can implement them until they become habits.

I achieve this result 60-80% of the time.
You are doing great, better than most at this Essential Skill. Consider new actions you can implement to improve your results. You already have the tools, taking a new approach when you face uncertain circumstances can improve your results even further. Hone in on your ability and make it work for you.

I achieve this result 80-100% of the time.

It must be said…you are awesome at this! The best way to focus this strength is to share it and teach it to others. Helping others to grow is the bonus round of your skill set. You will continue to improve through teaching and learning from the positive change in others. You can use the actions listed in Part Two of this book, along with your own experience to facilitate those discussions.

Charting Your Top Priorities

In this chapter you will find two worksheets titled "My Top Priorities". We recommend you focus on four results that need improvement (two results per worksheet). Once you implement these actions over a period of time, 3-6 months, you can go back, re-assess and focus on new Top Priorities. There are additional worksheets available at the back of this book.

Start by reviewing your answers and transferring your results that ranked in the 0%-20% range. If you only have two results in that range, transfer those to your priority list and then choose to from your 20%-40%, followed by your 40%-60% results and so on, for the remaining priorities. Ultimately you should be able to document four Top Priorities. Don't worry about the rest; there will be time to improve those areas after tackling your critical issues.

Write your Top Priorities on the left side of each box, leaving the right side (action plan) empty for now. Here is an example:

My **Top Priorities**

Over the next 3-6 months I will work to achieve the following result.	These are the Actions I will take to focus my efforts.
I am able to work across departmental silos to get things done and get the support needed to accomplish my team member objectives.	Action 1
	Action 2
	Action 3

Once you establish your Top Priorities, read through Part Two of this book. It details 100+ actions you can take to achieve positive results. Once you have read through the full section, go back and complete the right side of this form, developing a detailed action plan that you can commit to.

My Top Priorities

Over the next 3-6 months I will work to achieve the following result.	These are the Actions I will take to focus my efforts.
	Action 1 >
	Action 2 >
	Action 3 >

Over the next 3-6 months I will work to achieve the following result.	These are the Actions I will take to focus my efforts.
	Action 1 >
	Action 2 >
	Action 3 >

My Top Priorities

Over the next 3-6 months I will work to achieve the following result.	These are the Actions I will take to focus my efforts.
	Action 1
	Action 2
	Action 3

Over the next 3-6 months I will work to achieve the following result.	These are the Actions I will take to focus my efforts.
	Action 1
	Action 2
	Action 3

PART TWO

100+ ACTIONS SUCCESFULL PROFESSIONALS TAKE

Skill #1: Leadership

Skill #2 Management

Skill #3 Job Performance

Skill #4 Communication Skills

SKILL #1
LEADERSHIP

Leadership is a soft skill that allows you to move forward, at your desired speed, in your career and in your personal life. It is essential in anyone's development whether you want to lead a business, department, team, or your own destiny. It is about getting people to follow your lead & respect your input; this is vital no matter what you do.

Successful Leaders share five KEY attributes:

1. Their Direct Employees are interested in, and act on what they say.
2. Their Peers are interested in, and act on what they say.
3. Their Boss is interested in, and acts on what they say.
4. They ensure their objectives are known AND understood by everyone in the organization.
5. They can articulate objectives of others throughout their organization and understand how those objectives support their own.

Leadership, as a skill, boils down to the ability to accomplish your goals through others, on your terms and with *their* enthusiasm. In order to develop this Essential Skill you need to achieve all five Key Attributes within your work environment.

- It is not enough to have the respect of your boss without earning the respect of your peers.
- *Knowing your objectives* is important, but your ability to *inspire action in your employees* is essential to accomplishing them.

Anyone can develop this skill and it can be used everywhere, however what will set you apart is how well you integrate all five Attributes into your everyday **actions**, make them your **goals**, and transition those goals into **results**.

This chapter details potential actions you can take to generate positive results for each of the Key Leadership attributes.

Be sure to highlight the actions you are interesting in and determine if they should be added to your Top Priority Action List.

Leadership Goal #1: My Direct Employees are interested in, and act on what I say.

Why is this important?

Leadership by 'control' is not really leadership because as soon as you are not around, people will do their own thing. Your goal as a leader is to ignite a passion in others, a passion to accomplish your goals because they are interested in them and make them their own. If you get your direct employees to have an interest in what you say, they will become partners in the challenge to get the right things done.

Potential Actions:

- Show an interest in what your employees have to say by spending regular one-on-one time with them discussing objectives, ideas, individual challenges & accomplishments, as well as to reiterate team & business goals.
- Ask for their input whenever possible on your own work and the work of your team.
- Provide updates on group results, with detailed explanations; make time to teach them. Your value as their leader is not only about setting direction, it is about becoming a central knowledge point and sharing your direction from that advantageous position.
- Train your employees through your dialog and by providing examples; speak to be understood, not heard.
- Follow-up with your employees after your discussions to ensure they understand & don't have any lingering questions.

Leadership Goal #2: My Peers are interested in, and act on what I say.

Why is this important?

Leadership lies within one's ability, not their position in the hierarchy. No matter what your job, if you can ignite teamwork in your peers, you will develop the support system you need to get things done. This is not about being liked, instead it is about being respected as an expert in your field, a valued contributor to the group and a thought leader within your team.

Potential Actions:

- Show an interest in what your peers have to say, not only about their work, but be open to what they say about yours as well.
- Make an effort to understand what they do and how it relates to your job, offering solutions to make collaborative improvements.
- Try to implement continuous improvement efforts in your work/team and share the ideas with your peers. If they see your forward movement, they will be more aware of your activities in order to stay 'in the know'.
- Offer your help to your peers. By proactively giving your time, support or a concession to your peers, they will be more inclined to pay attention to <u>your</u> needs.
- Share your goals and results with your peers to keep them in the loop on your work. By regularly sharing information you project yourself as leader, not someone who holds information close to the chest.

Leadership Goal #3: My Boss is interested in, and acts on what I say.

Why is this important?

Leading 'Up' is an important aspect of any leader. In an environment where your role is typically to take direction, if you can shape the relationship to the point where your suggestions become the directions of your boss, then you have mastered your communication skills and are ready to make the next step in your career.

Potential Actions:

- Always try to give your boss credit for your work. He or she hired you and is responsible for setting your direction, so in some respect they should get credit. The more credit you give them, the more you will get from them.
- Make an effort to stay informed on actions and activities taking place outside of your team and make recommendations as to how your group can participate and bring value to other areas of the company.
- Always, always, always get your work done as they have asked for it prior to making a recommendation to do it differently. You can go the _extra_ mile to put your stamp on things, but first fulfill your responsibilities per your boss's viewpoint. (That's why it's called **extra**…it must be in addition to the task at hand.)
- Establish regular meetings with your boss to discuss your work, your accomplishments and the activities that you are focused on for the next period of time. These can be 15-30min reviews, once a month or once every other month. Your proactivity will be refreshing to your boss and will give you a stage to voice your ideas. (Do not use this time to ask for anything like a promotion or raise.)
- Stand up for what you believe during one-on-one discussions. It is not good to pander to your boss if your goal is to be respected. Be prepared and be confident in your own ideas/points of view. State your case with examples and external feedback, be respectful and factual. Once you have gone through this process and the answer or decision is "no", move on.

Leadership Goal #4: My objectives are known AND understood by everyone in the organization.

Why is this important?

True Leaders are not shielded by their direct employees or immediate teams; they are the voice all employees hear and feel a connection with. Whether you are the company president, middle manager or high potential employee, your ability to connect with people throughout your company and spread your message of goals, timelines, importance of your work and the impact they have on it, will determine how well you lead. Your results will prove this to be true. Think about the impact of this. Consider three scenarios:

1. Your objectives stay within your own confines.
2. Your objectives are filtered by others.
3. Your objectives are embedded in everyone.

Which of these three scenarios would you expect to generate the best results when you are trying to achieve a specific result within a specific timeframe? If you want to be effective, no matter what your role in the organization, you must be able to achieve scenario number 3.

Potential Actions:

- Start by defining your objectives for your own clarity. **What, When, Why & How** are the key details you need to compose in simple, understandable language. It is a good exercise for your own use. If you can't answer these questions yourself, you will not be able to engage others to act on them.
- Take the time to identify **Who** is impacted by your objectives and **Where** they are located. If you are going to reach the people needed to help you succeed, you must make this distinction in order to put an appropriate communication plan together.
- Establish a repeatable message that can be pushed by you and by others. It can be a presentation, a monthly report, a quarterly newsletter, or a weekly memo. But it must be tangible and "referenceable" for the people

you identified in the Who and Where of your organization.

- Listen to feedback throughout your organization on the message you are sending. Is it understood? The best way to learn this is by directly asking for others to explain your objectives and timelines back to you, along with an evaluation of what they need to do to support those objectives.

- Modify your plan if and when you need to. It is important to be flexible with your message in order to ensure it is understood and in order to incorporate new knowledge into your planning. When people feel you understand them and are not just sending out unjustifiable objectives, they will be more likely to buy into your vision, and help you achieve it.

- Communicate changes so that people do not find your message 'unjust'. When you change your action plan, direction, or objectives, the changes must be meaningful and justified in order to achieve buy-in. You don't want people to think that the path keeps changing because the plan isn't working. Instead, communicate the roadblock you are faced with and the solution to overcome that roadblock. This approach will resonate with people by showing that you are focused and innovative.

Leadership Goal #5: Throughout my organization I can articulate the objectives of others and how well those objectives support my own.

Why is this important?

A leader builds an infrastructure to support their vision. Without understanding if that infrastructure is sound at all levels, successful implementation is at risk. Leadership is taking vision to the next level of implementation…don't stop at idea generation, that's not leadership.

Potential Actions:

- Create a flowchart of your organization: how does work flow from the time of customer retention, to product/service delivery and follow-up, what are roadblocks, what are objectives.
  This is important to understand in order to foresee conflicts with your strategy and objectives. This foresight will help you prepare for discussions about any changes that need to be made in order to support your strategy. Without this knowledge you may have people agree to your strategy but not follow through on it.

- After presenting your objectives, request a formal discussion/presentation from each department defining their own objectives in support of your own.

- Create short-term incentive plans in line with overall objectives, but broken down by department. You will get a clear picture of their priorities, measureable and shared.

- Share objectives throughout your company. By providing a full circle plan in a visible document, your organization will see the impact their role plays in the bigger picture.

- Communicate with employees other than managers, direct reports and peers. In order get a clear picture of what others see as their objectives; you must establish a line of direct communication with people you don't typically have regular access to. Once you feel confident that your message is understood here, you will know your infrastructure is sound.

SKILL #2
MANAGEMENT

Whether you are currently a manger, or want to be one eventually, the ability to take on responsibly and coordinate multiple variables: people, processes, timelines, personalities, objectives, etc.... in order to get things done, is an essential aspect of your development.

Successful Managers share five KEY attributes:

1. They are consistent in their requests and expectations of others.
2. They praise others for their accomplishments both privately and publically.
3. They understand overall company goals and create their own clear action plan, not only for themselves, but also for their team.
4. They are able to work across departmental silos to get things done and get the support needed to accomplish team member objectives.
5. They regularly provide constructive feedback and set both group & individual continuous improvement targets for their team.

Management is an Essential Skill because it enables you to guide, support, motivate and persuade others to achieve a common goal. It also establishes your position as a resource, valued support system, and well-rounded mediator to break down barriers and build bridges to achieve better results, faster and more efficiently.

This chapter details potential actions you can take to generate positive results for each of the Key Management attributes.

Be sure to highlight the actions you are interested in and determine if they should be added to your Top Priority Action List.

Management Goal #1: I am consistent in my requests and expectations of others.

Why is this important?

If you are going to guide and judge someone's performance, you must first be incredibly clear as to what your expectations are. This is one of the biggest downfalls of managers and the biggest complaints from employees about their boss. Inconsistent or unclear expectations lead people to make their own assumptions, work independently of the team, or lose focus on generating optimum results. However, if your requests are clear and consistent, you have a tool by which you can measure an employee's ability to get things done. You also have a foundation to manage them, help them adjust and grow in their job in order to achieve your goals.

Potential Actions:

- Put it in writing! Gather your thoughts, define what you want to accomplish and who you want to delegate each task to, timelines, objectives, etc. and write them down. This is not only for your employees to reference; it is for you to remember what you have asked for.
- Meet with your team and/or employees to present your requests/expectations, as well as provide them with a written document for them to take. Be sure to ask and answer questions to ensure they understand with clarity what is being asked of them.
- Agree to a regular follow-up system with your employees. This can be in the form of a monthly report, weekly email updates, team meeting presentations, etc. The key is that the feedback is anticipated and regularly shared.
- Set performance objectives around specific expectations, or based on their ability to complete your requests. Your method depends on your type of business, or working level of your employees. For example:
  - "Complete product launch xyz by March 1st"- Gives employees autonomy to accomplish tasks as they see fit as long as the end product is completed on time.
  - "Reduce the average time to complete quality reviews form 15 days to 7 days" –This is a traceable measurement where you judge an average result using several inputs.
- Manage the amount of objectives you give to each employee. You don't want to overwhelm your employees with too many requests. They will lose focus and you won't achieve your end result without keeping your employees focused. By tracking what you ask for, you can ensure your requests, expectations, and timeframes are realistic.

Management Goal #2: I give praise to others for their accomplishments BOTH privately and publicly.

Why is this important?

If you want your employees to get things done for you, as well as be motivated to do more, you need to make sure they see and hear your acknowledgement of their efforts. Public and private praise is seen and heard. As a matter of fact, when employees hear their boss consistently giving them credit and not taking it as their own, especially when nobody is looking…moral improves and employees believe that their work is getting noticed to the point where they want to continue to do great things in order to continue to get noticed. This works for everyone, employee, co-worker & boss. It is human nature to like feeling appreciated…when you go out of your way to do it for others, they will in turn go out of their way to help you succeed the next time.

Potential Actions:

- Show an interest in what others are doing by asking them questions about their work, as well as about their ideas. Try to understand them and then help them promote their work internally by telling others about the value they are bringing to the group.
- When giving presentations to anyone, including your own boss, give credit to others that helped you with ideas or any work associated to what you are doing.
- Implement quarterly or yearly rewards for members of your team. This can be monetary or in the form of an award.
- Ask their opinion on your work. Sometimes praise comes in the acknowledgement that you trust their judgment.
- Give others more responsibility-delegate more important work to them with the caveat that you are respectful of their abilities and want them to take on more because of it.

Management Goal #3: I understand the overall company goals and have created a clear action plan for myself and my team to support that effort.

Why is this important?

Sometimes company goals are clear from 10k feet, but it is difficult to take them and make them real for your own job and for your team. It is important to take the time to define how they relate to you.

✓ What can you do differently to work in line with company objectives?
✓ What objectives should you target for yourself and your employees in order to help achieve overall objectives?

By doing this effectively your team can make a positive impact and you have talking points to review with your own boss as to the value your team provides to the company.

Potential Actions:

- Sit down with your boss and review overall company goals: budget, strategy, financial objectives, actionable missions & timelines. Make sure you walk away with a clear understanding of big picture objectives, as well as how your boss sees them impacting your work. If it is not clear from this discussion, ask to have it clarified by someone else in the company hierarchy. (Maybe your boss should do this as well if he or she is unable to provide clarity.)
- Itemize, in writing, the actions and priorities you and your team already do that are linked to the overall company objectives. Make sure that these items are highlighted as the "right path".
- Create a list of new actions and objectives you and your team should begin to take in order to positively impact overall company goals. Highlight these items as "new targets".
- Review current actions and objectives that you and your team have in place that may no longer make sense. Sometimes we do things because we always have, by putting these items in a bucket and evaluating whether or not they should be continued, you can free up time and resources to focus on objectives to move the company forward, and beyond stagnant. Highlight these items as "phase out".
- Meet with your employees and your boss to review the overall company goals, as well as your new list of priorities and impactful work you plan to do to help progress the company objectives. Make sure you publicize your results through weekly and/or monthly reports. Being vocal about your objectives and the value you and your team bring will help you get approval for additional resources needed to accomplish your goals.

Management Goal #4: I am able to work across departmental silos to get things done and get the support needed to accomplish my team member objectives.

Why is this important?

As a manager, people depend on you to break down barriers and build necessary bridges required to accomplish tasks and achieve targets. Relationship building is a very important part of your job, not only among your team, but also across teams, departments and hierarchies. Your ability to work cross-functionally, will set you apart as a professional and effective manager.

Potential Actions:

- Map out your department's workflow defining their internal suppliers (the people they receive work from) and their customers (the people they provide work to). Understanding the process flow will help you to build relationships with the right people.
- Meet with your department's suppliers and customers to understand if your team is meeting their needs. Work with them to define how the working relationship could be streamlined and made more efficient.
- Work with your team to identify the roadblocks they face. Create a priority chart, with their input, and use this list as your action plan to make your team more effective. Maybe you need more resources or additional training, maybe you need to eliminate ineffective practices, maybe you need to revise processes, or maybe you need to mend fences/create bridges with other departments.
- Work with other managers to set collaborative objectives & appoint key points of contact to improve process flows. Make sure you report results of these objectives to all parties and maintain the dialog on a regular basis.
- Educate your team on priorities of the business, your department and other departments within the company. The better understanding people have about the value and importance of their work, and the work of others, the more willing they are to proactivity help the larger team.

Management Goal #5: I regularly provide constructive feedback and set both group & individual <u>continuous improvement</u> targets for my team.

Why is this important?

Maintaining the status quo is not good enough. Management's role is to set the direction of their department in support of overall company goals, create a cohesive unit focused on achieving specific targeted results & finally, ensure continuous improvements in processes, people and benchmarks (what you hold your team accountable to). By setting both group & individual <u>continuous improvement</u> targets, you will be able to create a successful forward moving culture.

✓ A continuous improvement target is a specific result you aim to achieve which is above and beyond the current norm; ensuring actions to set new benchmarks.

Potential Actions:

- Conduct a formal lessons learned review with your team. This process can be applied to completion of projects or achievement of monthly results. By taking the time to discuss as a team, what worked and what didn't work, along with actions that can be taken to change processes for future projects or future month activities, you are able to implement step changes to get you further along your success path. Stop doing things that are not working well and establish things that work well as new standards. This process will generate new ideas for evaluating better ways of doing things.
- Implement an informal lessons learned process for your team. This is like an idea submission box, but with

a twist. In order for an idea to be considered "continuous improvement" it must be associated with a reduction of some sort. If we do this, we can stop doing this… An informal lessons learned process is a great way to build a culture of improvement.

- Education is another continuous improvement objective that can be individual or group based. You can require employees to achieve certifications, or take courses to advance their knowledge on processes, technologies, or concepts. Keep in mind that the goal is not only to learn, but also to implement this knowledge in their work and the work of the team. You can use the lessons learned process as a follow-up to training.

- Review your team's benchmarks and set the standards higher. Choose things that are measurable in your work: deadlines, work hours, costs, output, sales measurements (pricing, volumes), claims. Some of these benchmarks are already linked to your team's objectives, and some are not. The goal here is to keep raising the bar. If you already consistently hit targets, raise them. If you have a work standard, improve it. Always keeping in mind that you may need to make some investments to achieve new levels. It is your job as manager to ensure you secure resources necessary to improve.

- Gather team feedback from team members, other departments and customers where possible. You can do this by creating a survey that itemizes the deliverables of your team, as well as some soft points such as availability, collaboration, and responsiveness. Have them rate your group as a whole. It's not about singling any individual out; it is about setting standards for the team that you can hold each person accountable to achieve. Gather results and put a plan in action with your team to improve results. Make sure it is a very specific plan with actions and targets defined. Follow-up with monthly results vs. targets and drive these changes forward.

SKILL #3
JOB PERFORMANCE

Being proficient, innovative, respected and resourceful in your job are all tangible skills necessary for your professional development. This, combined with your soft skills makes you a full package ready to advance in your career.

Successful Individuals that excel in their Job Performance share five KEY attributes:

1. They proactively implement new & improved ways of doing things on a regular basis.
2. They earn a reputation as the go-to-person for their area of expertise, in AND outside of their department.
3. They take on leadership roles for projects outside of their current job duties.
4. They understand the full business cycle, both processes and people that interact with their area of responsibility.
5. They spend more time focusing on perfecting their current job vs. proving their ability for the position they really want to be promoted to.

Excelling in Job Performance is an Essential Skill no matter what position or job function you hold. It is the benchmark for your career growth and provides a unique opportunity to raise the bar for you as an individual performer.

This chapter details potential actions you can take to generate positive results for each of the Key Job Performance attributes.

Be sure to highlight the actions you are interested in and determine if they should be added to your Top Priority Action List.

Job Performance Goal #1: I proactively implement new & improved ways of doing things on a regular basis.

Why is this important?

Staying both current on trends and innovative with your approach to work, are two very important aspects of any high potential employee. Proactive means you are the one to seek out improvements. It is not a measurement of how well you follow direction when a change takes place, instead, you are the one proposing positive change. This is important because it shows you understand the ins and outs of your job to the level that you can modify (improve) it without negative impact. Your actions here show others that you are vital to the forward movement of the company.

Potential Actions:

- Conduct a "does this make sense?" evaluation of your job. It is a simple way to begin to make improvements. Too often we do things a certain way because that is how its always been done, regardless if it makes sense to continue doing it that way. Asking yourself this question will create a mindset for improvement. Be sure to make changes, creating new, more efficient standards for your job.
- Spend some time with your internal customers and suppliers (these are the people you work with from other departments either receiving work from them or passing it along after you completed yours). Collaborate with them to create a workflow diagram and define what can be done to improve the process flow between you. This process should generate collaborative ideas for change.
- Initiate or conduct a team brainstorming meeting to evaluate how well your work performance & objectives align with overall company goals. Determine 2-3 things you can do to contribute to the success of overall objectives.
- Stay up-to-date on job trends by reading articles, taking courses/seminars & working towards certifications or degrees in your field. Learning new concepts naturally leads to changing your job process.
- Find one or two mentors who can guide you to new ways of doing things. A mentor is typically someone who has been there, done that, and now sits at a higher level in the organization (whether yours or a different company all together). They can be a great resource to bounce your ideas off of before you implement them.

Job Performance Goal #2: I am the go-to-person for my area of expertise, in AND outside of my department.

Why is this important?

Being the go-to person means three things: you are resourceful, accessible & a good communicator. These are very powerful tools for any successful individual. Developing them around your current job is a great way to build your brand and get recognized in your organization for future growth. Providing yourself as a resource outside of your department means that you have developed relationships with other departments and management levels to the point where they come to you for support.

Potential Actions:

- Knowledge is power, and so is sharing it with others. Share your work & results up, down, sideways & across the isle…What better way to get known than to proactively share your results with people? If you take the approach that you want them to know what you are working on just incase they can use the information to help their own work effort, people will be interested to follow your progress. Make sure you take some time to formulate your report so that it speaks for you, and to your audience, communicating your effectiveness.

- Become the bridge between your department and others to ensure workflows are streamlined and challenges are overcome quickly. An informal approach is to try to help out when problems arise, but a more proactive approach is to initiate this liaison service prior to problems happening. Develop the bridge infrastructure between yourself and other willing designees within departments you work with. Then try to have the process formalized by the rest of your team, including your boss.

- Talk with people; get to know your co-workers and others within your company. Develop a rapport and make sure it includes not only personal niceties, but professional discussions as well. By creating regular dialog you will have more opportunities to engage in conversation that pertains to your job, helping others and providing resources.

- Take your work to the next level whenever you are asked to do something or when you are working with others. The point here is to complete the task at hand, but then offer something in addition. A different perspective or additional information you think would be useful. This type of action will raise expectations for future work, and make people realize that they can come to you for ideas.

- Compile knowledge. Not everyone, actually, very few people, have the ability to understand the full spectrum of the company, or even a microcosm of it. Try to learn as much as you can about the business and how your work relates to it and other parts of the company. If you communicate that knowledge to others during casual conversations, people will come to you to brainstorm opportunities because you may have insight into how well ideas will be accepted in the company.

Job Performance Goal #3: I take on leadership roles for projects outside of my current job duties.

Why is this important?

Leadership is a skill that advances you. It pulls people toward you and provides opportunity to coordinate activities from multiple vantage points. If you seek opportunities to lead outside of your current team, you will open the door to those vantage points, creating a larger group of people that, when the time is right, will acknowledge your leadership skills and help you succeed. Creating a reputation as a leader can be a great asset for your career.

Potential Actions:

- Facilitate a meeting to improve communication within your department. Creating a dialog on communication issues is a great leadership tactic within your own team, allowing you to lead a topic separate from your specific job.

- Volunteer outside of work to help a charity or sit on a board. This work is rewarding as you "give back," but it is also a good way to see yourself in a leadership role outside of your business persona.

- Establish a training session on your department, or specifically on your job, for other employees in your company to attend. Talk with other department personnel to see who is interested in helping you prior to setting this up. You can present an explanation of department metrics, communication processes or just a general overview. Educating people on your department is much appreciated internal training. Teaching is leading when you bring value to the group, helping them to work better together.

- Become a mentor. Talk with your HR leader to set this up. They can recommend some people that may be in need of mentoring within your organization.

- Ask your boss for leadership opportunities. It may be as simple as facilitating a meeting, leading a project group or coordinating efforts with other departments or customers. Putting yourself out there as being interested in these opportunities will open the door when one presents itself.

Job Performance Goal #4: I know the processes and people that interact with my area of responsibility both before and after my job takes place in the business cycle.

Why is this important?

Your ability to get things done in your job depends on how well you communicate, understand processes and manage problems that occur. By having a deep understanding of your workflows, both in and outside of your department, as well as the people your work touches, you will be able to improve your effectiveness and efficiency levels…freeing you up to grow and take on new opportunities.

Potential Actions:

- Reconfirm the expectations your boss has for you. Are your goals and objectives aligned with your work? Take the time to answer these questions and modify your actions based on what you find.
- Get to know what your employees are working on, where they excel and where they are hitting roadblocks. Work with them to create bridges that improve workflow and streamline processes.
- Establish key people in each area of the business so that there is a constant balance created between ease of working together and implementing changes necessary to improve cross-departmental issues. (Key Points of Contact…Accountability)
- Take a course or seminar on different aspects of your business: accounting, marketing, finance, operations, etc… By getting some formal training on all aspects of the business, you will be able to develop a more well-rounded view and communicate with other groups with a clearer understanding.
- Set up a meeting with everyone your work connects to. Develop a flowchart of the business and determine together what can be done to improve the flow. The goal is to reduce the amount of steps it takes for all parties in the flow chart; collectively becoming more efficient.

Job Performance Goal #5: I spend more time focusing on perfecting my current job vs. proving my ability for the position I really want to get promoted to.

Why is this important?

You must succeed before you can be successful! If you want to be taken seriously for the next stage of your career, focus on being great during this one. Your boss and your organization will acknowledge your abilities and be more open to promoting you if you are a proven performer. You should not fear being pigeonholed in your current job, instead create an environment where you advance the job itself, promotion will be natural.

Potential Actions:

- Automate as much of your work as possible. This can be through process improvements, improved communication or elimination of unnecessary steps. The more efficient you can work, the more time you will have to do other things. And the easier it will be for someone to replace you when there is opportunity for you move on…and up, in your career
- Delegate portions of your work to other, more capable people. Don't hang onto things that others can do better. If you have the resources, such as employees who work for you, don't forget to utilize them. Train them to take on more and reduce the reliance on yourself to get everything done.
- Ensure everything is on time or early, as well as done incredibly well. The quality and reliability of your work is important. Do not leave any question whether or not the company can count on you.
- Over deliver on results. If you are asked to do something, do it per the request, and then make it better.

Your ideas are easier to sell up if you first respect up. It may mean that you complete two pieces of work, that is ok, this process will not take forever. By showing respect for the people asking for the work (giving them what they requested), and then saying "Here are some other ideas I thought you might be interested in and here's why" they will be open to your ideas because you already fulfilled their need. They are not clouded by doubt... they will see your skill as going above and beyond, respecting you for it & soon asking for your input in advance.

- Add on responsibility without being asked. Once you streamline your process, reduce workload through delegation, and create a reputation of high quality performance, you will have time to improve your job by taking on additional responsibility, implementing programs or ideas, collaborating with other departments, etc.... Essentially, advancing your job to the next level. Then, prior to your next performance review, you can request your position be reviewed for a promotion since your level of responsibility has increased. You are setting yourself up for growth after proving you've earned it; your company will not want to disappoint you

SKILL #4
COMMUNICATION SKILLS

You can have great ideas, amazing abilities and productive relationships, but if you don't have the skill to communicate effectively, get buy in and mobilize others, you are limiting how much you can actually accomplish. Great Communication Skills give you an edge in everything you do as a manager, leader & individual contributor by understanding your audience and projecting your message in a way that others can understand, buy into and act upon.

Successful individuals who Master Communication Skills share five KEY attributes:
1. They regularly get buy-in and approval for their ideas.
2. They are comfortable expressing themselves using multiple communication vehicles.
3. They can properly articulate the concepts of others, and often do so to help them get buy-in for their ideas.
4. They routinely share information, both good and bad, with the intent to engage others, solve problems and continuously improve.
5. They proactively engage everyone in the company with positive dialog no matter their reaction or response.

Excellent Communication Skills are an Essential Skill for everyone, benefiting both your work and private life. Having the ability to listen, understand, engage and be understood are vital to getting things done effectively. Some people excel on communication skills alone, in the short term this is possible, but when you combine all 4 Essential Skills into your professional development, you will create sustainable growth for your career, accomplish more and realize greater fulfillment in your achievements.

This chapter details potential actions you can take to generate positive results for each of the Key Communication Skill attributes.

Be sure to highlight the actions you are interested in and determine if they should be added to your Top Priority Action List.

Communication Skills Goal #1: I regularly get buy-in and approval for my ideas.

Why is this important?

The more often you take the time to explain your thoughts & ideas to the extent that others agree and go along with you, the more likely you will be revered as an expert in your field or job junction. Over time their wiliness to listen will improve and the time it takes to influence others will shorten because your words will have more power - giving you the time & ability to take on more responsibility. The challenge is being able to convince others, overcome obstacles and sell your ideas.

Potential Actions:

- Include others in your work, getting their input prior to formalizing your approach to whatever it is you are working on. This will enable you to take inspiration from them and then use it to help explain your ideas back to them. By feeling included, they will have a vested interest in going along with you.

- Approach your concept from all angles prior to presenting it to anyone. Try to determine roadblocks or opposing opinions so you can address those before they are brought to your attention. If your audience feels comfortable that you have done your due diligence, they will feel more secure in their decision to agree with you.

- Understand the objectives of your audience, the people you want to approve your ideas, and incorporate those objectives into wording of your own. Make sure there is a common alignment and vocalize the overall benefit that will take place once you are allowed to move forward.

- Test your concept by getting feedback from someone you trust before presenting it to those you are seeking approval from. Sometimes getting impartial feedback is a good way to vet your ideas and improve your ability to present them clearly.

- Seek buy-in individually before you officially approach a group for approval of your ideas or concepts. This means sitting down one-on-one with individuals that are part of the approval process. Ask questions, and feel them out as to how your approach may be perceived. Take their feedback to heart and incorporate modifications into your final approach. For example, if you are presenting to the management team, and you already privately discussed your concept with two of the members, your official presentation will already have two advocates prior to walking in the room. This will help you feel more comfortable about the reaction of the group because you have already developed supporters who will help you field questions from the others.

Communication Skills Goal #2: I am able to comfortably express myself using multiple communication vehicles (writing, presentations, discussions).

Why is this important?

People learn differently, some listen, some are more visual, some prefer to read a report. Bottom line, you must be prepared to reach your audience through whatever means works best for them, not you. Developing your skills to communicate effectively over multiple mediums gives you the ability to reach a diverse group, in addition, it provides an opportunity to send a *consistent* message without sounding repetitive and losing the interest of your audience.

Potential Actions:

- Practice, practice, practice. When you have a message to deliver, a request to make or a direction to give, try creating it in multiple forms. Create a PowerPoint presentation, write a proposal or report, and prepare an in person discussion. When you present your idea, try using more than one form and see what gets the best response. Continue to practice this approach until your skills improve.

- Train. Take a class or webinar on presentation skills or public speaking. Even if you are comfortable with your skills, brushing up is always a good idea.
- Rehearse your message so that it becomes fluid, not planned. The more you rehearse you will be able to be agile during your presentations and discussions. That means you can answer questions, get your message across and always stay focused on what it is you are trying to accomplish.
- Test your message. Get feedback from someone or several people you trust prior to expressing yourself to your target audience. Use this feedback to modify your approach if necessary.
- Spread your message so it is not forgotten. Don't say something and expect it to be remembered and understood. Communicating effectively means you take the extra step to ensure the right follow-up takes place and that what you said has the impact you intended. By spreading your message consistently using multiple mediums and taking every opportunity to reiterate what you had to say, you are increasing your effectiveness.
- Plan follow-up. Make sure to articulate both verbally and in writing what the next steps will be, who is accountable for what tasks, as well as timing. This includes your own accountability. Then make sure you track this activity to ensure success.

Communication Skills Goal #3: I can properly articulate the concepts of others, and often do so to help them get buy-in for their ideas.

Why is this important?

Communication is not only a skill, it is an asset. If you are good at it and share it with others by helping them to communicate more effectively, you will develop a reputation for being a good listener, collaborator and team player. Long term, your network will grow to respect you, value your opinion and increase their loyalty; you become a better leader.

Potential Actions:

- Focus on listening and encouraging people to share their ideas with you. The more you know and get people to open up to you, the more of an asset you will be to your organization. Make sure to repeat and rephrase the ideas of others to ensure you understand them.
- Give credit to others all the time. This makes people trust you and as this trust grows, they will be more willing to share their ideas with you. Giving credit should not only be on a formal basis, but on an informal basis as well. When you sing the praises of others, emphasize their skills, and promote their value, the benefits come back to you far more than trying to take credit for everything yourself.
- Show an interest in what others are working on or responsible for. Ask questions; try to understand their goals and challenges. Don't judge, just learn. This process will help you to become more well-rounded and also help you to build productive relationships.
- Offer yourself as a sounding board to those you work with. A random, "hey if you ever want some feedback I am here to help" goes a long way. The more you develop your relationships and make this offer, the greater the likelihood people will come to you for help.
- Seek to collaborate across departments in order to build a better workflow or business model. Find out how your work impacts that of others and work with them to continuously improve your own activities. This process generates teamwork and provides a stage for you to lead positive changes in your organization.

Communication Skills Goal #4: I routinely share information, both good and bad, with the <u>intent</u> to engage others, solve problems and continuously improve.

Why is this important?

Intent is just as important as consistency when it comes to effective communication. Your audience will sense the difference between *pushing information because you have to* vs. *sharing information to include and engage them.* This practice will open doors to collaboration and give you a vehicle to get noticed for your leadership and job skills. Engaging others and moving them forward through your actions, communication and ideas is a leadership skill and a much different approach to the typical process people take for things such as monthly reports and meetings.

Potential Actions:

- Develop a complete understanding of your work activity. Define what works well, and what could benefit from being improved. By understanding the big picture, you can focus on bits and pieces of improvement while managing the impact of any change. Sharing your activities and knowledge with colleagues, employees and your boss will show your value and ensure a true benefit the company.

- Hold your reaction to complications, conflicts or bad news. Instead of engaging in these activities as they happen, spend your time investigating the cause from all perspectives, developing a cross-functional solution agreeable to all parties and an implementation plan to correct the situation so that it will not happen again. Once fully vetted, share the information and resolution with the intent to teach as well as set the stage for others to handle difficult situations in the future.

- Create a series of metrics to manage and track your activities and results. By establishing benchmarks & goals, implementing improvement plans & monitoring results, you ensure your message has purpose and relates to the business. Good or bad news, you can show you are in control and set the course for what happens next.

- Create a regular and easily understood platform for sharing information. It can be a monthly report, weekly meeting, daily email or quarterly newsletter. There are endless ways to share information, but the important thing is to keep it consistent and ensure the content clearly shows the past, present and future. Your goals are to teach and reassure.

- Ask for feedback on your message. Proactively engaging people to find out if they have questions on your reports is a good way to continue the dialog, ensure they are paying attention and determine if there is anything else you can do to communicate more effectively.

Communication Skills Goal #5: I proactively engage everyone in the company with positive dialog no matter their reaction or response.

Why is this important?

A bad attitude can kill your career; a positive one can propel it. It is a simple concept, but a difficult one to live up to, especially when you are faced with a stressful situation or negative reactions from people. As difficult as it can be, it is important that you take the high road and create a positive atmosphere around yourself and your team. Think about it. Who would you rather work with, someone who focuses on making positive things happen no matter how difficult the situation, or someone who focuses on the negative and leaves a sense of insecurity when things don't go well? Who would you want to hire or promote? No matter how well you do your job, communicating your positive attitude will give you an advantage for promotions. Needless to say, being positive will help you to enjoy your job more.

Potential Actions:

- Go out of your way to say hello to people of all levels within your company. Ask them how their day or week is going, how a presentation went, or just tell them it is good to see them. If they don't respond, don't be offended; instead, continue to offer your hello with enthusiasm every time you see them. Eventually you will leave your mark as a positive influence and they may even respond positively to you.
- Look people in the eyes and be attentive when speaking with them, and when they are speaking with you. Avoid doing email, taking phone calls or responding to other disruptions during conversations or meetings.
- Repeat and rephrase what people say to show them that you are paying attention. Offer additional information if you can bring value to their ideas.
- Try to give credit to people on a regular basis whether they are there to receive it or not. People will see you as trustworthy if they witness your ability to share success.
- Ask questions of others in an effort to educate yourself, not to prove them wrong. Take a humble, educational approach to your questioning and be grateful to others for sharing their knowledge with you.
- If someone is rude to you, don't argue back, just remain professional and stick to your points. Your goal is to be heard and to be known as the calming force in your organization.
- Avoid participating in negative dialog, instead propose potential solutions to problems and offer to help implement those solutions.

PART THREE

WHAT'S NEXT

Commit to Your Actions & Chart Your Progress

Establish a Process for Continuous Improvement

Additional Workbook Pages

COMMIT TO YOUR ACTIONS & CHART YOUR PROGRESS

Having goals is not enough, you must commit to your actions in order to achieve them. The most challenging part is to determine what those actions should be, then hold yourself accountable for implementing them.

By now you have developed a general framework for your professional development, established your strengths & documented those areas that need improvement. The next step is to COMMIT TO YOUR ACTIONS by writing them down.

This is often the most challenging part for many professionals. You have to make a choice to implement the low-lying fruit, or choose actions that stretch outside of your comfort zone. One solution is to try a combination of the two.

- You can start by going back through PART TWO of this book and highlight the actions that seem attainable (low-lying fruit). Highlight low-lying fruit in one color, and the stretch actions in another.
- Next, document a combination of the two on your "Top Priorities" worksheet to the right of your target results. Choose three actions you can commit to and hold yourself accountable for. Here is an example:

My **Top Priorities**

Over the next 3-6 months I will work to achieve the following result.		These are the Actions I will take to focus my efforts.
I am able to work across departmental silos to get things done and get the support needed to accomplish my team member objectives.	**Action 1**	Set up & lead a monthly meeting with managers from marketing, customer service & operations to establish collaborative objectives for our teams and review progress.
	Action 2	Work with my team to map out our existing workflow, identify roadblocks and develop a more streamlined approach to achieve our targets.
	Action 3	Work with other department mangers to assign key personnel within each group responsible for collaborating, solving problems and making decisions.

Once your Priorities and Actions are completed you are ready to start making them real. Here are some tips to help you get started:

- Reference your Top Priority chart every day either by posting it on your wall or replicating it on your computer or smart phone. Getting a quick reminder is a good way to keep your mind focused and aware of opportunities to implement your actions.
- Set your calendar to represent your commitments. If you committed to meet with other mangers, peer group, or employees, set these meetings up in advance on your calendar, along with inviting the appropriate people.
- Prepare for your discussions. Take the time to think about what you want to say, how you want to say it and what the follow-up from your meeting should be. This is your opportunity to lead your own change, by leading the way others perceive you.

Keep in mind your success will take time and effort. Try not to get overwhelmed by changing too much too soon. Stay focused on a few priorities until they become habits. Then go back and choose your next set of Top Priorities and Actions to commit to. Your cycle of professional development should be continuous.

The next pages of this book are worksheets you can use to CHART YOUR PROGRESS. For every Action you have Committed to, it is important to document the individual results you see. Here is an example:

Action: Work with my team to map out our existing workflow, identify roadblocks and develop a more streamlined approach to achieve our targets.

Result: We identified that product trials were dependent upon breaks in the operations schedule. If we are busy they don't happen within a reasonable timeframe and we lose out on hot leads. We worked with operations to schedule a standard trial run period into the weekly operations schedule. Now we can use this standard trial timeframe as a selling point with customers.

The above example depicts an action and result related to improving Essential Skill #2: Management. As you chart your progress use the appropriate worksheet. There is a different worksheet for each Essential Skill. This will allow you create a clear visual of your results.

- Continue to reference your success until your actions become habits.
- Use your learning experiences as teaching opportunities for your own employees.
- Use your documented progress as reference points to discuss with your boss during performance reviews.

Leadership Progress Report

A c t i o n

R e s u l t s

A c t i o n

R e s u l t s

A c t i o n

R e s u l t s

Management Progress Report

A c t i o n

R
e
s
u
l
t
s

A c t i o n

R
e
s
u
l
t
s

A c t i o n

R
e
s
u
l
t
s

Job Performance Progress Report

Action

Results

Action

Results

Action

Results

Communication Skills Progress Report

Action

Results

Action

Results

Action

Results

ESTABLISH A PROCESS FOR CONTINUOUS IMPROVEMENT

Great Managers and Leaders incorporate a lessons learned, or continuous improvement process into their teams and organizations. It keeps them agile and ahead of their competitors. Successful individuals take the same approach to their careers, proactively charting their course, advancing their abilities and measuring their success. It all starts with the active development of 4 Essential Skills.

Congratulations, you are on your way to professional success! Here are some things to keep in mind as you develop your continuous improvement process, document your efforts & advance your Essential Skills...

1. Plan a consistent Skills and Progress Review once a week, every other week or no later than once per month. This repetition will keep your goals at the forefront of your mind and your actions consistent. You can start by setting up a repeated calendar invite to ensure your actions become habits.
    a. Use this time to document your results, evaluate your action plan & determine if you should be adding additional goals to your TOP PRIORITY list. Keep in mind that you should update your TOP PRIORITIES only when you are sure your actions have become habits and your desired results have become the new way others perceive you.

2. Consider using this Essential Skills Process as a management tool for your team. You can rate your employee along with his or her own personal assessment. Together you can establish targets and coach them throughout the year. If you use personal objectives as part of your compensation system, this is a good way to help them achieve those goals.

3. Put Essential Skills development at the forefront of your organization by making it part of your company culture. The more people you have taking part in this process, the more supportive the working environment will be for everyone.

4. Make sure to document your success. Changing your approach to people, as a manager, leader and individual contributor is not easy to do. You've already taken the first step by reading this book. Opportunity awaits you...it is up to you make it your own reality.

5. At the end of each year take the assessment again. Have you made your actions into habits? Where should you focus next? Continuous improvement is important to become the best you can be, your Professional Growth depends on it.

6. Continue to develop new ideas & ways of doing things. Your potential is infinite if you *want* it to be!

ADDITIONAL WORKBOOK PAGES

Keep your effort going. Only you can hold yourself accountable for your professional success. Make these tools work for you.
- Lisa Woods

The following pages are extra documents for your use:

- TOP PRIORITIES worksheets

- Essential Skills progress reports

My Top Priorities

Over the next 3-6 months I will work to achieve the following result.	These are the Actions I will take to focus my efforts.
	Action 1
	Action 2
	Action 3

Over the next 3-6 months I will work to achieve the following result.	These are the Actions I will take to focus my efforts.
	Action 1
	Action 2
	Action 3

My Top Priorities

Over the next 3-6 months I will work to achieve the following result.	These are the Actions I will take to focus my efforts.
	Action 1
	Action 2
	Action 3

Over the next 3-6 months I will work to achieve the following result.	These are the Actions I will take to focus my efforts.
	Action 1
	Action 2
	Action 3

My Top Priorities

Over the next 3-6 months I will work to achieve the following result.	These are the Actions I will take to focus my efforts.
	Action 1
	Action 2
	Action 3

Over the next 3-6 months I will work to achieve the following result.	These are the Actions I will take to focus my efforts.
	Action 1
	Action 2
	Action 3

Leadership Progress Report

A c t i o n

R
e
s
u
l
t
s

A c t i o n

R
e
s
u
l
t
s

A c t i o n

R
e
s
u
l
t
s

Management Progress Report

A c t i o n

Results

A c t i o n

Results

A c t i o n

Results

Job Performance Progress Report

Action

Results

Action

Results

Action

Results

Communication Skills Progress Report

A c t i o n

R
e
s
u
l
t
s

A c t i o n

R
e
s
u
l
t
s

A c t i o n

R
e
s
u
l
t
s

ABOUT THE AUTHOR

Lisa Woods, President & CEO ManagingAmericans.com

Lisa, a thought leader in management and leadership, founded ManagingAmericans.com in 2011 after 20+ years successfully leading and driving growth in the corporate world. Her objective is to help mentor and develop professionals to be better leaders, managers, team players and individual contributors in a "do-it-yourself" learning environment using unique & practical tools to support the process. With a B.A. in Corporate Communication and an M.B.A., Lisa's career spans from Global Marketing to General Management and has worked all over the world. Her publications include "4 Essential Skills for Leaders, Managers & High Potentials" © 2013, "The Cross Functional Business: Beyond Teams" © 2015, and "Action Item List: Drive Your Team With One Simple Tool" © 2016.

9 780615 810836